First Words and Pictures

My Busy Day

By Ruth Owen, Emma Randall and Sophie Murphy

Aberdeenshire

Published in 2017 by Ruby Tuesday Books Ltd.

Copyright © 2017 Ruby Tuesday Books Ltd.

Editor: Mark J. Sachner
Production: John Lingham

Photo Credits:
Photographs courtesy of Shutterstock

British Library Cataloguing In Publication Data (CIP)
is available for this title.

ISBN 978-1-911341-65-9

Printed in Poland by L&C Printing Group

What's Inside the Book?

yawn

clock

It's Morning!

toothpaste

brush hair

toothbrush

brush teeth

toilet

flush

toilet roll

wash hands

soap

towel

potty

nappy

5

shirt

buttons

cardigan

Time to Get Dressed

belt

zip

jeans

hoodie

vest

knickers

dress

T-shirt

pants

shorts

jumper

skirt

trousers

Can you find the matching pair of socks?

eat

drink

Time for Breakfast

cereal

bowl

porridge

8

boiled egg

spoon

sticky

jam

egg cup

toast

toaster

spread

peanut butter

pour

crumpet

cup

orange juice

melted butter

9

tie laces

boots

shoe

Off to School

car

car seat

seat belt

coat

scarf

hat

bus

scooter

walk

bike

zebra crossing

STOP

school

classroom

Welcome to Our School

friends

teacher

pencil

book

alphabet

numbers

table

chair

reading

writing

painting

13

sand

gardening

Things We Do

puzzle

Duck

soft play

guitar

bongos

drum

xylophone

shakers

making music

tambourine

15

wash hands

lunch

Time for Lunch

water

yogurt

tuna

cheese

carrot sticks

jacket potato

peas

sandwich

fruit

mashed potato

fish fingers

cucumber

omelette

milk

MILK

ONE PINT (473mL)

sharing

hugging

Things We Do and Feel

hands up

helping

laughing

crying

happy

How do you feel today?

sad

excited

shy

running

dancing

On the Move!

kick

football

yoga

swimming

arm bands

swimsuit

trunks

bat

ball

hoops

What is your favourite sport or game?

throw

catch

21

library

supermarket

Places We Go

playground

park

duck pond

doctor

dentist

nurse

birthday party

vet

kitten

washing machine

cooking

Around My Home

dishwasher

lawn mower

cushions

tablet

sofa

screen

phone

laptop

keyboard

vacuum cleaner

television

remote control

wash hands

family

Time for Dinner

spaghetti

stir-fry

biryani

pakora

beans

grapes

plate

knife

fork

salad

chicken

beans on toast

sausages

broccoli

sweetcorn

sleepy

bath

Time for Bed

brush teeth

bedtime story

slippers

bunk beds

pyjamas

teddy bear

pillow

kiss

duvet

goodnight

29

Tips and Ideas

Look ✓ Read ✓ Talk ✓ Discover ✓ Learn ✓

This book is designed to help you and your child get the best learning experience possible. We suggest that you make yourselves comfortable within a quiet environment and allow your child to hold the book and turn the pages. When you and your child are reading the book, pause to allow your child to *read* a word or ask questions about the pictures and words.

Page 5: After your child has used the toilet or potty, allow him or her to pull up their pants or knickers. Then ask your child what they need to do next. If your child does not know, remind him or her that it's important to wash their hands to stop germs spreading.
1) Wet hands with clean water.
2) Apply soap.
3) Rub and scrub for 20 seconds.
4) Rinse with clean water.
5) Dry with a towel.

Pages 6-7: Ask your child what items of clothing he or she is wearing today. Do the clothes have buttons or a zip?

Pages 8-9: Give your child some fruit cut into small pieces. Ask the child to make a face from the different fruit shapes. When the face is complete, eat it all up!

Pages 10-11: Ask your child how he or she got to school today and discuss the journey. You can use toy cars or buses as props during your chat. Point out the pictures of the car seat and zebra crossing. Talk about keeping safe – for example, why should a child sit in a car seat, or why do drivers stop at traffic lights? If the child walked to school, discuss the importance of lollipop ladies and men at zebra crossings.

Pages 16-17: Ask your child to point to or say their favourite foods on these pages, and on pages 8–9 and 26–27. Ask them what other foods they like to eat. Discuss with your child the importance of making the right food choices. Download a free healthy-eating chart and a fun activity about making food choices from:

www.rubytuesdaybooks.com/firstwords

Pages 18-19: Discuss what is happening in the pictures with your child. Ask questions such as:
• How do you think the girls who are hugging feel?
• How do you think the girl who fell over feels now that her friend has helped her?
• What do you think could have made the boy cry? Do you think that a hug might make him feel better?

Page 25: Find an old phone or laptop and remove the battery. Allow the child to use this technology to mimic what he or she sees in everyday life. You can use your own phone to join in with the role play.
Ask questions such as:
• Who are you talking to on the phone?
• What are you doing on the laptop?
• What happens when you tap on the keyboard?

Pages 28-29: Look at the pictures and ask your child about their bedtime routine.
• Do you have a favourite bathtime toy? What is it?
• Do you share a bedroom with anyone?
• What do you wear for bed?
• Who reads you a bedtime story?
• Do you have a teddy bear or a special blanket?

Busy Day Activities

Make a Feelings Chart

Go online to find photos that show different facial expressions – for example, happy, sad, scared, shy, unwell, excited, angry, embarrassed, sleepy. Print, cut out and write the feelings word beneath the face. (You can also draw faces.) Stick Blu Tack to the back of each face. Take an A4 piece of card and write "How am I feeling today?" at the top. Pin the card to a wall or stick it to the fridge. Ask your child how he or she is feeling at different times of the day. The child can say or point to the relevant face, and then stick the face beneath the question.

Let's Make Music!

Create your own musical instruments with your child. Make a drum out of a saucepan and hit it with a wooden spoon. Create a shaker using a plastic bottle that's half-filled with uncooked rice or pasta.

Go On a "Places in My Community" Hunt

Create a tick list using photographs of different places in your local community – for example, a school, church, mosque, park, supermarket, zebra crossing, doctor's surgery, fire station, restaurant or garage.

When you're out and about, encourage your child to say when they spot the place. Tick the place on the list and then discuss with your child what happens in that building or community area.

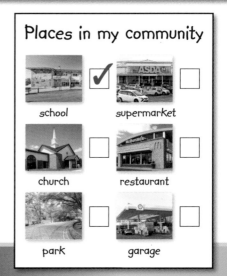